Model Fire Engines
Full-Color Reference Guides to Die-Cast Emergency Vehicles®

by
ANDREW BENZIE

for information about other books in this series:
www.ModelFireEngines.com

Published by Andrew Benzie Books: www.andrewbenziebooks.com

Copyright © 2017, 2024 Andrew Benzie. All rights reserved.
No part of this publication may be reproduced, distributed or transmitted in any form or by any means, or stored in a database or retrieval system without prior written permission of the author.
"Siku" and the Siku logo are registered trademarks of Sieper GmbH, used with permission.
This unauthorized book is derived from the author's independent research.

First edition January 2017. Second edition v2.0 June 2024.
ISBN: 978-1-941713-31-0

Photography, cover & book design by Andrew Benzie.

Andrew Benzie Books
Martinez, California

ABOUT THIS BOOK

Author Andrew Benzie began collecting die-cast model emergency vehicles in the 1970s when his grandparents gave him his first **Corgi** and **Dinky** toy fire engines. In this book Andrew presents his collection of over 200 die-cast emergency vehicles produced between 1963 and 2017 by **Siku** (Germany). Updated second edition with appendix June, 2024.

The models appear in alphabetical order by vehicle make, and detailed information about each model is included below each photo. Every effort has been made to maintain accuracy in the listings—please send any comments or corrections to **andrew@andrewbenzie.com**.

Thank you for purchasing this book. For updates (including new Siku releases) and information about other books in this series, please visit **www.ModelFireEngines.com**.

ABOUT SIKU MODELS

The German firm **Siku** (founded in 1921 by Richard Sieper) produced their first model fire engine (#121, 1:60 scale) out of plastic in 1950, and began making Zamak (zinc-alloy) die-cast models in 1963 for the **V Series** ('V' for 'vehrkehrs' modelle, or 'traffic' model).

The **Super Series** models (1:55 scale) debuted in 1975 and have been popular with collectors ever since. The smaller **Club Series** (usually 1:87) was introduced in 1990 and was merged into the Super Series in 1993. Manufacturing moved from Germany to China in 1994.

The **Siku Junior** line was launched in 1998 and consists of larger (1:20 scale) detailed plastic trucks. The **Super Classic** range of classic old-timer fire engines (1:50 scale) was added in 2005 to complement the contemporary models in the Super Series. **Siku World** was launched in 2013 and consists of plastic buildings and street tiles including a model fire station (2015).

Plastic Fire Engine #121, 1950, 1:60

High quality production, attention to detail and working parts are hallmarks of Siku models. The company also owns the well-known HO scale plastic model producer **Wiking**. For more information about Siku, visit **www.siku.de**.

1957   1970   1971   1972   1976   1994

Special thanks to my family for putting up with all this. **Dedicated to** firefighters around the world. **References**: Siku website, catalogs, dealer brochures and model boxes; *Feuerwehrmodelle* by Thomas Herminghaus (1987); *Miniature Emergency Vehicles* by Dr. Edward Force (1985); *The Siku Story* by Ulrich Biene (2014); *Siku-Sammlerkatalog RAWE 2003* by Wilfried Raschke/Manfred Weise (2003).

FULL-COLOR REFERENCE GUIDES TO DIE-CAST EMERGENCY VEHICLES

Audi 100 #353/#1313, Arzt Notfalleinsatz, 1973-1974/1975, 1:60

Audi A4 Avant 2.5 TDI Quattro #1313, Feuerwehr, 2007, 1:55

Audi A4 Avant 3.0 TDI #1422, ADAC, 2014-2017, 1:55

Audi A6 1.9 TDI #1313, Feuerwehr, 2002-2003, 1:55

MODEL FIRE ENGIES: SIKU

Audi Q7 4.2 FSI Quattro #1429, Notarzt, 2008-2017, 1:55

Audi Q7 4.2 FSI Quattro #1429, Rettungsdienst, 2008-2017, 1:55

Audi Q7 4.2 FSI Quattro #1460, Feuerwehr, 2008-2012, 1:55

BMW 545i #1460, Feuerwehr, 2011, 1:55

FULL-COLOR REFERENCE GUIDES TO DIE-CAST EMERGENCY VEHICLES

BMW X5 #1432, ÖAMTC, 2011-2017, 1:55

BMW X5 #1466, Notarzt, 2011-2013, 1:55

BMW R 1100 RS Motorcycle #1324, ADAC, 1998-2000, 1:43

BMW R 1100 RS Motorcycle #1314, Feuerwehr, 2002-2004, 1:43

MODEL FIRE ENGIES: SIKU

BMW Motorcycle #1654 (from Fire Brigade Set #1654), 2016-2017, 1:43

BMW Motorcycle #1656 (from Fire Brigade Set #1656), 2016-2017, 1:43

Dodge Charger #1468, Fire Chief, 2011-2015, 1:55

Dodge Charger #1468, 2016-2017, 1:55

FULL-COLOR REFERENCE GUIDES TO DIE-CAST EMERGENCY VEHICLES

Dodge Viper #1434 (from Fire Brigade Set #7509), Feuerwehr, 2013, 1:55

Eurocopter BK-117 Helicopter #2228/#2539, ADAC, 1992-2000/2001-2005, 1:55

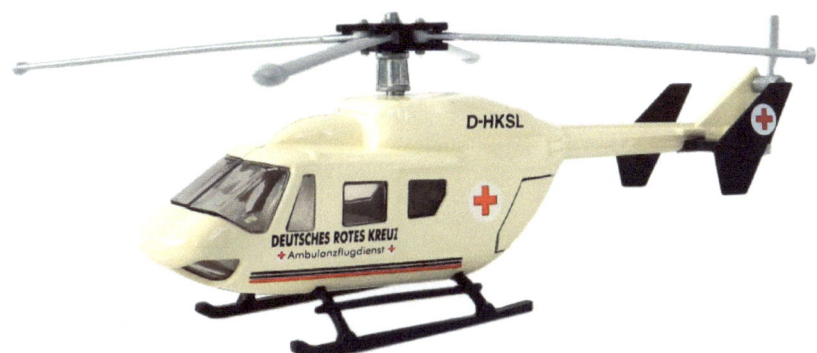

Eurocopter BK-117 Helicopter #2535, Deutsches Rotes Kreuz, 1995-1996, 1:55

Eurocopter BK-117 Helicopter #2614, Katastrophenschutz, 1993-1994, 1:55

Eurocopter BO-105 Helicopter #2222, Metro-Dade Fire-Rescue Air Rescue One, 1986-1997, 1:55

Eurocopter BO-105 Helicopter #2224, Feuerwehr, 1990-1994, 1:55

Eurocopter BO-105 Helicopter #831, ADAC, 1993-1995, 1:110

Eurocopter BO-105 Helicopter #832, Feuerwehr, 1993-1995, 1:110

FULL-COLOR REFERENCE GUIDES TO DIE-CAST EMERGENCY VEHICLES

Eurocopter BO-105 Helicopter #832, Rescue, 1993-1995, 1:110

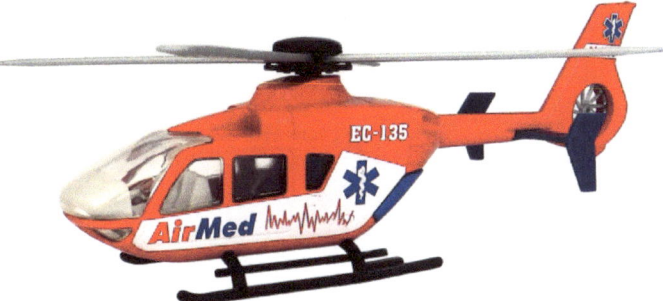

Eurocopter EC-135 Helicopter #2538, AirMed, 1999-2006, 1:55

Eurocopter EC-135 Helicopter #2539, ADAC, 2006-2017, 1:55

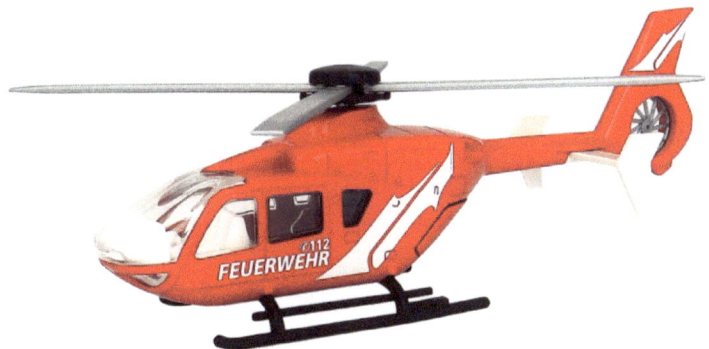

Eurocopter EC-135 Helicopter #2539 (from Fire Brigade Set #7509), Feuerwehr, 2013, 1:55

MODEL FIRE ENGIES: SIKU

Eurocopter EC-135 Helicopter #1850 (Rescue Service Set), ADAC, 2008-2017, 1:87

Eurocopter EC-135 Helicopter #1850 (Rescue Service Set), 2008-2017, 1:87

Eurocopter EC-135 Helicopter #1850 (Rescue Service Set), 2008-2017, 1:87

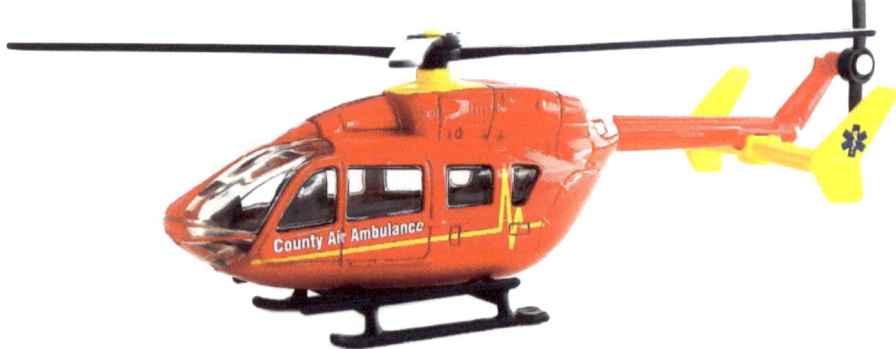

Eurocopter EC-135 Helicopter #1647, County Air Ambulance, 2008-2017, 1:87

FULL-COLOR REFERENCE GUIDES TO DIE-CAST EMERGENCY VEHICLES

Eurocopter EC-135 Helicopter #1647, Sécurité Civile, 2008-2017, 1:87

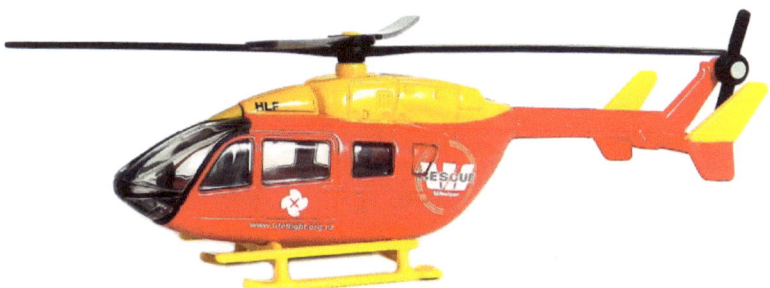

Eurocopter EC-135 Helicopter #1647, Westpac Life Flight, 2008-2017, 1:87

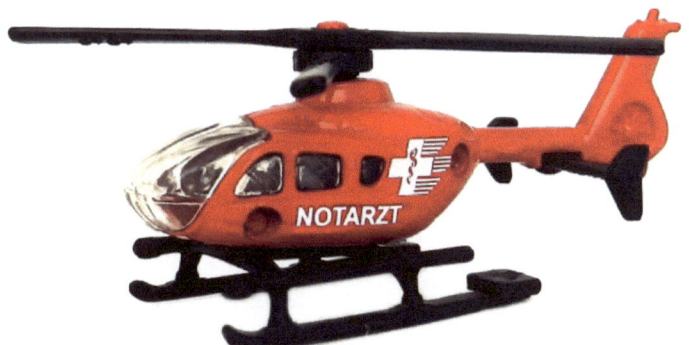

Eurocopter EC-135 Helicopter #856, Notarzt, 2001-2006, 1:110

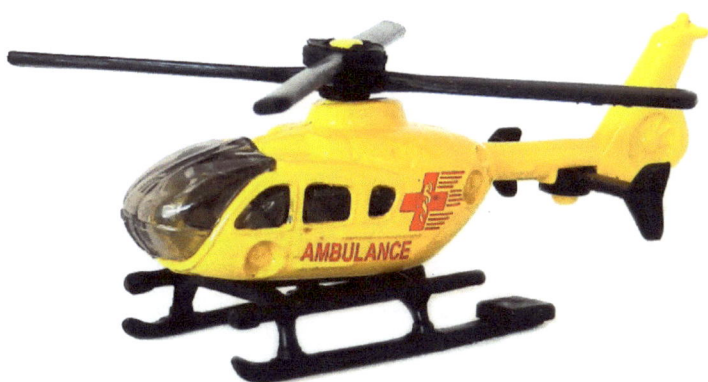

Eurocopter EC-135 Helicopter #856, Ambulance, 2007-2017, 1:110

Eurocopter EC-135 Helicopter #853, ADAC, 2004-2017, 1:110

Eurocopter EC-135 Helicopter #853, ÖAMTC, 2004-2017, 1:110

Faun Ladder #2924, 1992-1993, 1:55

Faun Crane #3127, Feuerwehr, 1985-1994, 1:55

FULL-COLOR REFERENCE GUIDES TO DIE-CAST EMERGENCY VEHICLES

Faun/Grove Crane #4110, Feuerwehr, 1986-1988/1992-1993, 1:55

Faun Crane #1326 (from Fire Engine Set #1661), Rescue, 2011-2017, 1:87

Ford Cargo Lowboy with Eurocopter BO-105 Helicopter #3719, ADAC, 1985-1997, 1:55

Ford Cargo Lowboy with Eurocopter BO-105 Helicopter #3719, Securite Civile, 1985-1997, 1:55

MODEL FIRE ENGIES: SIKU

Ford Cargo with Fireboat #2823, Pompiers, 1987-1988, 1:55

Ford Grenada 17M Turnier Kombi #V313, ADAC-Straßenwacht, 1970-1974, 1:60

Ford Grenada 17M Turnier Kombi #V342, 1973-1974, 1:60

Ford Grenada 17M Turnier Kombi Fire Chief #1617, 1975-1982, 1:55

FULL-COLOR REFERENCE GUIDES TO DIE-CAST EMERGENCY VEHICLES

Ford Galaxy 2.8i #1323, ADAC-Pannenhilfe, 1997-2000, 1:55

Ford Transit Van #V237, 1964-1971, 1:60

Hako Kehrmaschine Street Sweeper #2104, Feuerwehr, 2004-2006, 1:50

Liebherr Crane #2110, Feuerwehr, 2011-2014, 1:55

MODEL FIRE ENGIES: SIKU

Lamborghini Espada 400GT #V344/#1618/#1336, Fire Hunter, 1973-1974/1975-1977/1978, 1:60

Lamborghini Espada 400GT #V344/#1618/#1336, Fire Hunter, 1973-1974/1975-1977/1978, 1:60

Magirus Fire Engine #4114, Siku Super Classic, 2005-2017, 1:50

Magirus Auxiliary Fire Tender #4115, Siku Super Classic, 2005-2017, 1:50

FULL-COLOR REFERENCE GUIDES TO DIE-CAST EMERGENCY VEHICLES

Magirus Auxiliary Fire Tender #4115, SSC Club Model, Zivilschutz, Siku Super Classic, 2013, 1:50

Man TGA/Rosenbauer Fire Engine #2101, Feuerwehr, 2003-2009, 1:55

Man TGA/Rosenbauer Fire Engine #2101, Fire and Rescue, 2003-2009, 1:55

Man TGA/Rosenbauer Fire Engine #2101, SSC Club Model, Wasserrettung, 2009, 1:55

MODEL FIRE ENGIES: SIKU

Man TGA/Rosenbauer Fire Engine #2102, Feuerwehr, 2004-2009, 1:55

Man TGA Halfpipe Dump Truck #2103, Technisches Hilfswerk (THW), 2008, 1:55

Man TGA Skip Loader #2103, 2004-2006, 1:55

Mercedes-Benz 300E #1339, Notarzt, 1991-1994, 1:55

FULL-COLOR REFERENCE GUIDES TO DIE-CAST EMERGENCY VEHICLES

Mercedes-Benz 300E #1349, Feuerwehr, 1992-1994, 1:55

Mercedes-Benz 220C #1349, Feuerwehr, 1995-1997, 1:55

Mercedes-Benz 320C #1313, Feuerwehr, 2004-2006, 1:55

Mercedes-Benz 300E #1414, Notarzt, 2004-2006, 1:55

MODEL FIRE ENGIES: SIKU

Mercedes-Benz 190 'Binz' Ambulance #V233, 1964-1970, 1:60

Mercedes-Benz 1200 'Binz' Ambulance #306/#1613, 1970-1974/1975-1980, 1:60

Mercedes-Benz 200 'Binz' Ambulance #1613, 1981-1988, 1:55

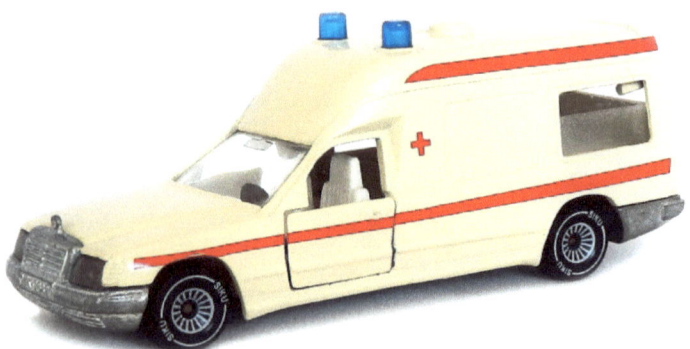

Mercedes-Benz 260E 'Binz' Ambulance #1630/#1718/#1928, 1989-1990/1991-1992/1993-1997, 1:55

FULL-COLOR REFERENCE GUIDES TO DIE-CAST EMERGENCY VEHICLES

Mercedes-Benz 260E 'Binz' Ambulance #2880, Feuerwehr, Siku Special Series, 1990-1993, 1:55

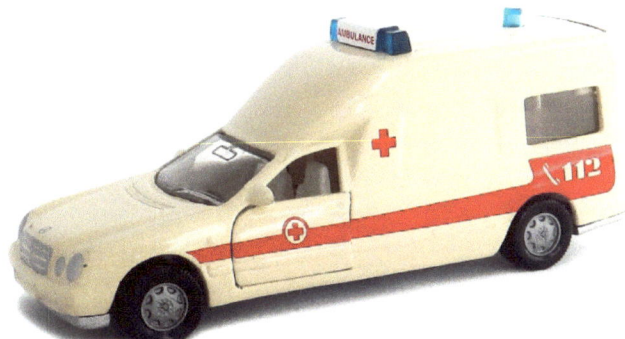

Mercedes-Benz 290E 'Binz' A2002 Ambulance #1931, 1998-1999, 1:55

Mercedes-Benz 290E 'Binz' A2002 Ambulance #1931, 1999-2008, 1:55

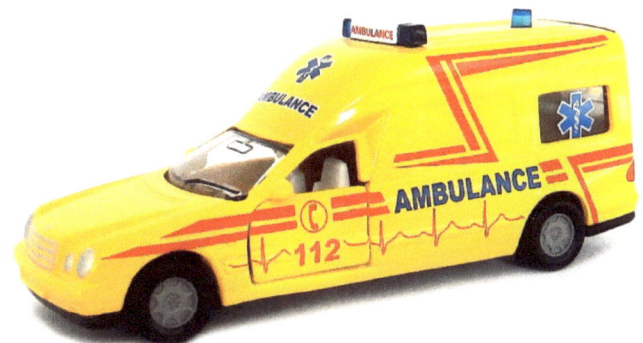

Mercedes-Benz 290E 'Binz' A2002 Ambulance #1931, 2008-2009, 1:55

MODEL FIRE ENGIES: SIKU

Mercedes-Benz 290E 'Binz' A2003 Ambulance #2107, Rettungsdienst, 2010-2012, 1:55

Mercedes-Benz 290E 'Binz' A2003 Ambulance #2107 (from Fire Brigade Set #7509), Feuerwehr, 2013, 1:55

Mercedes-Benz 290T #1364, Feuerwehr, 2000-2003, 1:55

Mercedes-Benz 280GE #1313, ADAC-Straßendienst, 1993-1996, 1:55

FULL-COLOR REFERENCE GUIDES TO DIE-CAST EMERGENCY VEHICLES

Mercedes-Benz 280GE #1344, Feuerwehr, 1983-1997, 1:55

Mercedes-Benz 280GE with Trailer and Boat #1923, Feuerwehr, 1989-1994, 1:55

Mercedes-Benz 405N Linienbus #2927, Feuerwehr, 1993-1994, 1:55

Mercedes-Benz 809D 'Binz' Rettungswagen #2011, Feuerwehr, 1987-1994, 1:55

MODEL FIRE ENGIES: SIKU

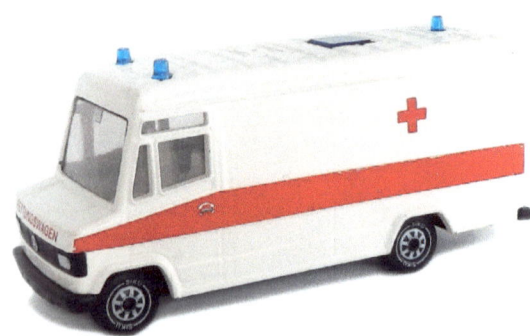

Mercedes-Benz 809D 'Binz' Rettungswagen #2015, 1993-1998, 1:55

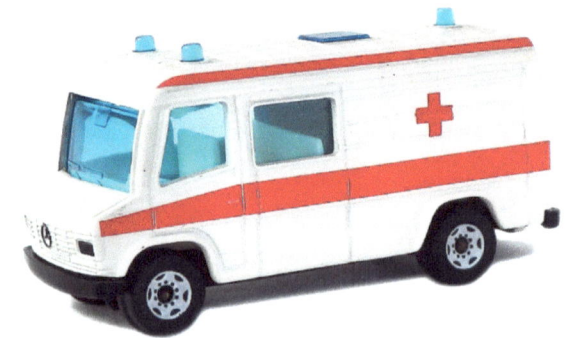

Mercedes-Benz 809D 'Binz' Rettungswagen #805, 1990-1995, 1:72

Mercedes-Benz A160 #1421, Feuerwehr, 2002-2003, 1:55

Mercedes-Benz Atego Fire Engine with Ladder #1841, Feuerwehr, 2005-2015, 1:87

FULL-COLOR REFERENCE GUIDES TO DIE-CAST EMERGENCY VEHICLES

Mercedes-Benz Atego Fire Engine with Ladder #2106, Feuerwehr, 2006-2015, 1:50

Mercedes-Benz Atego Water Cannon #1842, Feuerwehr, 2006-2011, 1:87

Mercedes-Benz/Metz DL30H Ladder #V261/#2815, 1966-1974/1975-1977, 1:60

Mercedes-Benz L406 #V292, , Unfall-Rettung, 1969-1974, 1:60

MODEL FIRE ENGIES: SIKU

Mercedes-Benz LA06 #V339/#2213, Wasserrettungfahrzeug, 1972-1974/1975-1980, 1:60

Mercedes-Benz LA06 #357/#2214, Unfall-Rettung, 1974/1975-1978, 1:60

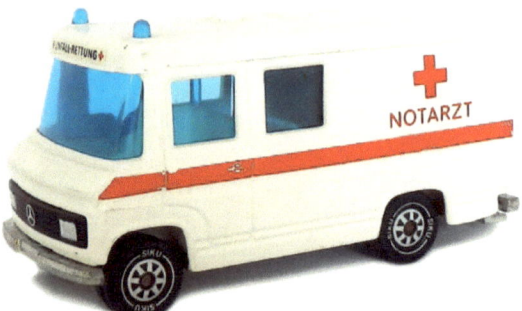

Mercedes-Benz LA06 #1911, Notarzt, 1975-1984, 1:60

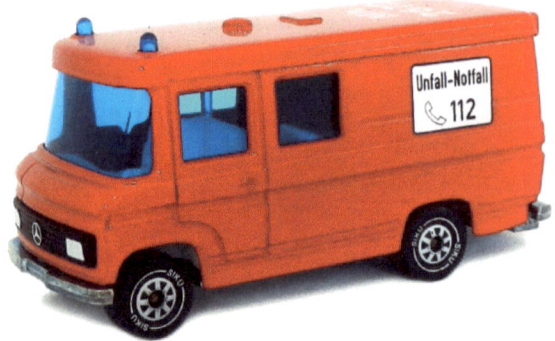

Mercedes-Benz LA06 #1911, 1985-1986, 1:60

FULL-COLOR REFERENCE GUIDES TO DIE-CAST EMERGENCY VEHICLES

Mercedes-Benz LN2 TLF Water Cannon with Trailer #2921, 1986-1989, 1:55

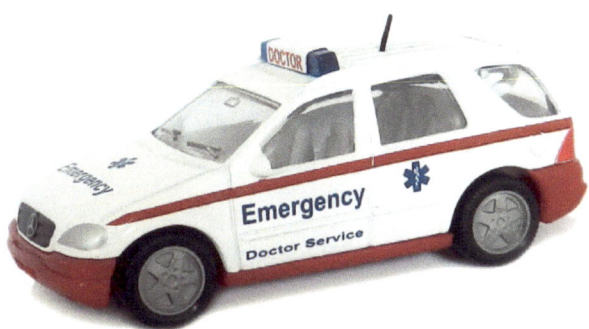

Mercedes-Benz ML320 #1414, Emergency Doctor Service, 2000-2004, 1:55

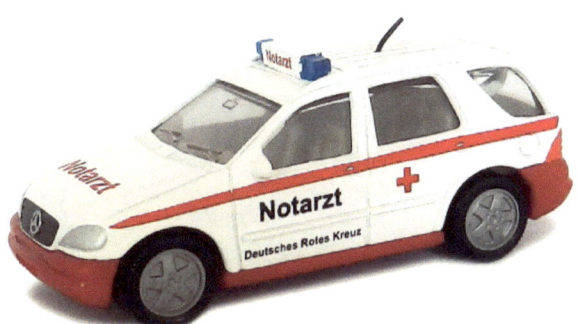

Mercedes-Benz ML320 #1414, Notarzt, 2000-2004, 1:55

Mercedes-Benz ML320 #1415, Direktionsdienst Feuerwehr, 2000-2004, 1:55

MODEL FIRE ENGIES: SIKU

Mercedes-Benz ML320 #1415, Kommando Berufsfeuerwehr Salzburg, 2008-2010, 1:55

Mercedes-Benz ML320 #1422, ADAC, 2002-2004, 1:55

Mercedes-Benz SK Ladder #812/#1015, 1990-1992/1993-1999, 1:72

Mercedes-Benz Actros Ladder #1015, 2000-2017, 1:72

FULL-COLOR REFERENCE GUIDES TO DIE-CAST EMERGENCY VEHICLES

Mercedes-Benz 2232 Fire Engine #2819, 1978-1991, 1:55

Mercedes-Benz SK Fire Engine #3780, Siku Special Series, 1990-1992, 1:55

Mercedes-Benz SK Ladder Truck #3433, 1996-2001, 1:55

Mercedes-Benz Atego Ladder Truck #3433, 2002-2003, 1:55

MODEL FIRE ENGIES: SIKU

Mercedes-Benz SK Rescue Truck #3512, Feuerwehr, 1992-1995, 1:55

Mercedes-Benz SK Snorkel #3720, Feuerwehr, 1990-1999, 1:55

Mercedes-Benz SK Simon Snorkel #827/#1019, 1992/1993-1999, 1:72

Mercedes-Benz Actros Simon Snorkel #1019, 2000-2007, 1:72

FULL-COLOR REFERENCE GUIDES TO DIE-CAST EMERGENCY VEHICLES

Mercedes-Benz SK Water Cannon #1034, Feuerwehr, 1995-1998, 1:72

Mercedes-Benz Actros Water Cannon #1034, Feuerwehr, 1999-2010, 1:72

Mercedes-Benz SK Water Cannon #3880/#3429, Feuerwehr, Siku Special Series, 1990-1993/1994-2000, 1:55

Mercedes-Benz 2232 Water Tender #2524, Sapeurs Pompiers, 1986-1990, 1:55

MODEL FIRE ENGIES: SIKU

Mercedes-Benz SK Water Tender #3511, Sapeurs Pompiers, 1989-2000, 1:55

Mercedes-Benz Skip Loader #2826, Feuerwehr, 1992-1994, 1:55

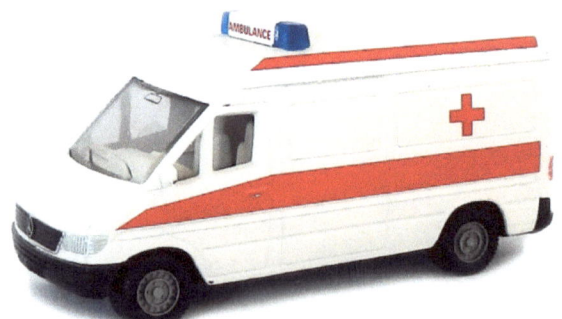

Mercedes-Benz Sprinter Ambulance #805, 1996-2007, 1:72

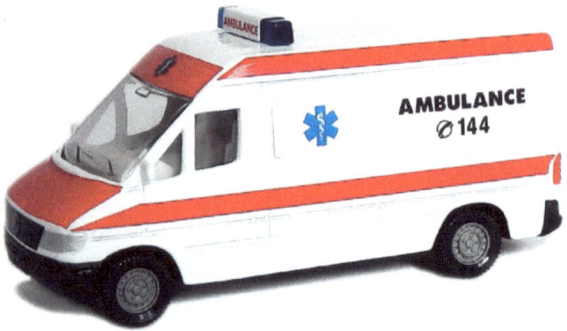

Mercedes-Benz Sprinter Ambulance #838, 2004-2009, 1:72

FULL-COLOR REFERENCE GUIDES TO DIE-CAST EMERGENCY VEHICLES

Mercedes-Benz Sprinter Ambulance #805, Rettungsdienst, 2008-2009, 1:72

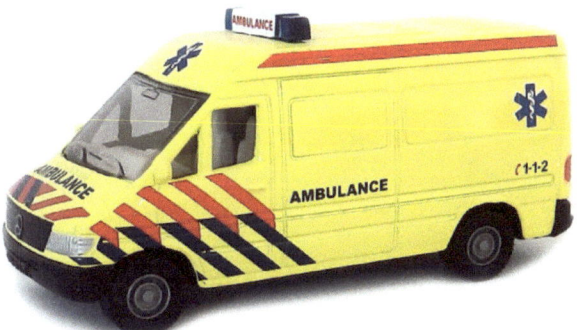

Mercedes-Benz Sprinter Ambulance #805, 2008-2015, 1:72

Mercedes-Benz Sprinter Ambulance #805 (from Fire Brigade Set #1656), 2017, 1:72

Mercedes-Benz Sprinter Ambulance #805 (from Fire Brigade Set #1656), Sapeurs Pompiers, 2013-2017, 1:72

MODEL FIRE ENGIES: SIKU

Mercedes-Benz Sprinter with Trailer and Boat #1638, Fire & Rescue, 2012-2013, 1:72

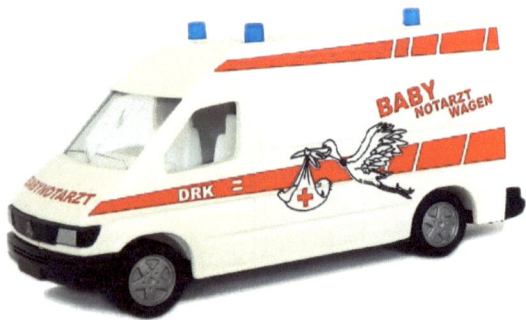

Mercedes-Benz Sprinter Ambulance #1932, Baby Notarzt Wagen, 1999-2001, 1:55

Mercedes-Benz Sprinter 312D Ambulance #2020, Feuerwehr, 2000-2003, 1:55

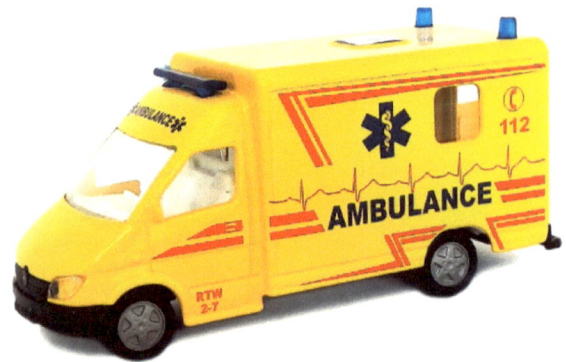

Mercedes-Benz Sprinter 312D Ambulance #2020, 2004-2005, 1:55

FULL-COLOR REFERENCE GUIDES TO DIE-CAST EMERGENCY VEHICLES

Mercedes-Benz Sprinter Ambulance #2108, Rettungsdienst, 2006-2017, 1:50

Mercedes-Benz Sprinter Ambulance #1850 (Rescue Service Set), Rettungsdienst, 2008-2017, 1:87

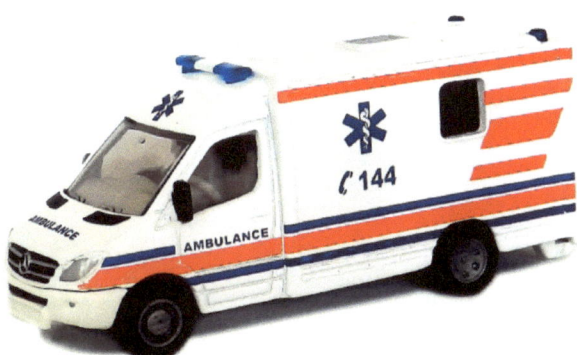

Mercedes-Benz Sprinter Ambulance #1850 (Rescue Service Set), 2008-2017, 1:87

Mercedes-Benz Sprinter Ambulance #1850 (Rescue Service Set), 2008-2017, 1:87

MODEL FIRE ENGIES: SIKU

Mercedes-Benz Sprinter Command Car #882, Feuerwehr, 2008-2009, 1:72

Mercedes-Benz Sprinter Command Car #882, Feuerwehr Einsatzleitung, 2010-2015, 1:72

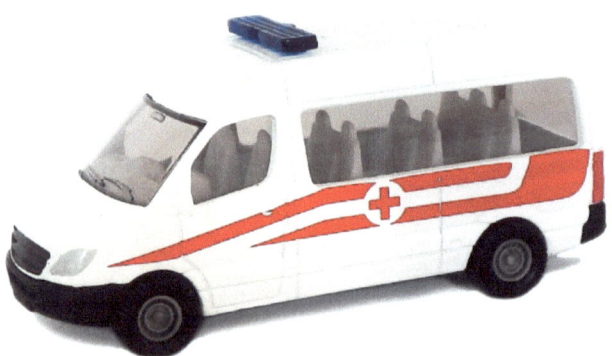

Mercedes-Benz Command Car Sprinter #805, 2016-2017, 1:72

Mercedes-Benz Sprinter Command Car #1082, Rescue, 2016-2017, 1:72

FULL-COLOR REFERENCE GUIDES TO DIE-CAST EMERGENCY VEHICLES

Mercedes-Benz Sprinter 6x6 Fire Engine #2113, 2015-2017, 1:50

Mercedes-Benz Sprinter 6x6 Fire Engine #2113, Feuerwehr, Interschutz Model, 2015, 1:50

Mercedes-Benz Sprinter 6x6 Fire Engine #2113, SSC Club Model, Technisches Hilfswerk (THW), 2015, 1:50

Mercedes-Benz Unimog 406 with Floodlight Trailer #2913, 1979-1984, 1:55

MODEL FIRE ENGIES: SIKU

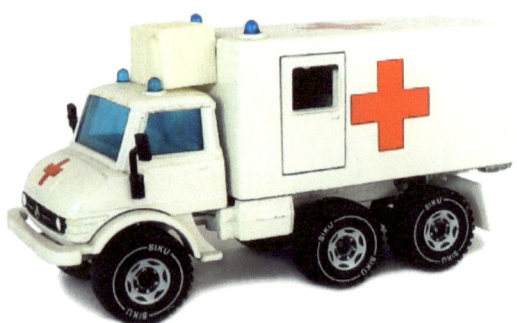

Mercedes-Benz Unimog 406 #2218, Saniätswagen, 1978-1985, 1:55

Mercedes-Benz Unimog 406 #2218, Sapeurs Pompiers, 1978-1985, 1:55

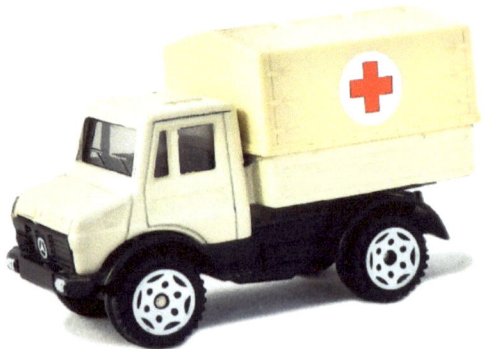

Mercedes-Benz Unimog U1500 #1026, Rotes Kreuz (Red Cross), 1994-1997, 1:72

Mercedes-Benz Unimog U1500 with Trailer and Boat #1517, DLRG (Lifeguard), 1998-1999, 1:72

FULL-COLOR REFERENCE GUIDES TO DIE-CAST EMERGENCY VEHICLES

Mercedes-Benz Unimog U400 #1068, Feuerwehr, 2006-2017, 1:87

Mercedes-Benz Unimog U400 #1068 (from Fire Engine Set #1661), Rescue, 2011-2017, 1:87

Mercedes-Benz Unimog U400 #1068 (from Fire Brigade Set #1656), Pompiers, 2013-2015, 1:87

Mercedes-Benz Unimog U400 with Trailer and Boat #1636, Feuerwehr, 2006-2017, 1:87

MODEL FIRE ENGIES: SIKU

Mercedes-Benz Unimog U400 #2710, Pompiers, 2005-2007, 1:55

Mercedes-Benz Zetros Fire Engine #2109, Fire & Rescue, 2013-2017, 1:50

Metz/Faun Airport Crash Truck #V332, Flugfeldlöschfahrzeug, 1972-1974, 1:60

Metz/Faun Airport Crash Truck #3411, Flugfeldlöschfahrzeug, 1975-1985, 1:60

FULL-COLOR REFERENCE GUIDES TO DIE-CAST EMERGENCY VEHICLES

Opel Astra Caravan #1320, ADAC-Straßenwacht, 1997-2000, 1:55

Porsche 928 #1339, Notarzt, 1979-1990, 1:55

Porsche Cayenne Turbo #1422, ADAC, 2005-2011, 1:55

Porsche Cayenne Turbo #1415, Feuerwehr, 2005-2007, 1:55

MODEL FIRE ENGIES: SIKU

Porsche Cayenne Turbo with Trailer and Hovercraft #2549, Rescue, 2014-2017, 1:55

Range Rover Vorausrüstwagen #1338, 1979-1989, 1:55

Rosenbauer Simba Airport Crash Truck #826, Feuerwehr, 1992-1997, 1:87

Rosenbauer Simba Airport Crash Truck #3513/#3722, Airport Berlin Tegel #7, 1992-1993/1994-1997, 1:55

FULL-COLOR REFERENCE GUIDES TO DIE-CAST EMERGENCY VEHICLES

Rosenbauer Panther Airport Crash Truck #1345, 2009-2012, 1:110

Rosenbauer Panther Airport Crash Truck #1889, 2009-2011, 1:87

Rosenbauer Panther Airport Crash Truck #2105, 2006-2014, 1:50

Rosenbauer Panther Airport Crash Truck #2105, Feuerwehr, 2006-2014, 1:50

MODEL FIRE ENGIES: SIKU

Scania 143H Low Loader with Eurocopter BO105 #1610, ADAC, 1995-2000, 1:72

Scania 143H Low Loader with Eurocopter BO105 #1610, Feuerwehr, 2001-2006, 1:72

Scania Water Cannon #1034, Feuerwehr, 2011-2017, 1:87

Scania Water Cannon #1034, Hamburg Airport Feuerwehr Fire & Rescue, 2011-2017, 1:87

FULL-COLOR REFERENCE GUIDES TO DIE-CAST EMERGENCY VEHICLES

Smart Car #1303, Feuerwehr, 2009, 1:55

Toyota RAV 4 #1465, Feuerwehr, 2009-2011, 1:55

Toyota RAV 4 #1466, Notarzt, 2009, 1:55

Volkswagen/Porsche 914 #346, ADAC Rennpolizei, 1973-1974, 1:60

MODEL FIRE ENGIES: SIKU

Volkswagen Amarok TDI #1467, Feuerwehr, 2011-2015, 1:55

Volkswagen Amarok TDI #1467 (from Siku World Fire Station Set #5502), Fire, 2015-2017, 1:55

Volkswagen Amarok TDI #1469, ADAC, 2012-2017, 1:55

Volkswagen Beetle 1300 #1324, ADAC-Straßenwacht, 1975-1984, 1:60

FULL-COLOR REFERENCE GUIDES TO DIE-CAST EMERGENCY VEHICLES

Volkswagen Golf #1312, ADAC-Straßenwacht, 1985-1990, 1:55

Volkswagen Golf #1437, Brandweer, 2014-2015, 1:55

Volkswagen Passat Variant #1342, ADAC-Straßenwacht, 1976-1984, 1:55

Volkswagen Passat Variant III #1312, ADAC-Straßenwacht, 1991-1995, 1:55

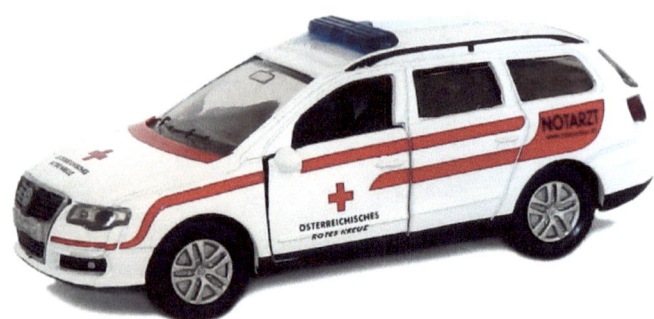
Volkswagen Passat Variant 2.0 FSI #1307, Osterreichisches Rotes Kreuz, 2008-2015, 1:55

Volkswagen Passat Variant 2.0 FSI #1461, Notarzt, 2008-2017, 1:55

Volkswagen Passat Variant 2.0 FSI #1464, Feuerwehr, 2009-2015, 1:55

Volkswagen Sharon #1368, Rettungsdienst, 2000-2002, 1:55

FULL-COLOR REFERENCE GUIDES TO DIE-CAST EMERGENCY VEHICLES

Volkswagen Tiguan #1422, ADAC, 2012-2013, 1:55

Volkswagen Type 181 'Thing' Einsatzleitwagen #1335, 1977-1982, 1:55

Volkswagen T2 Bus #V356/#1619, Malteser Hilfsdienst, 1974/1975-1978, 1:60

Volkswagen T2 Bus #1621, Military Ambulance, 1976-1979, 1:60

MODEL FIRE ENGIES: SIKU

Volkswagen T2 Bus #1315, Autobahn-Streckenwagen, 1975-1988, 1:60

Volkswagen T2 Bus #1347, Feuerwehr, 1990, 1:60

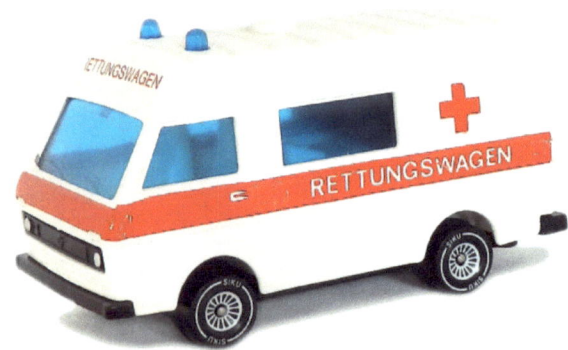

Volkswagen T3 LT28 #1623/#1711, Rettungswagen, 1979-1989/1990, 1:55

Volkswagen T3 Transporter #1343, 1982-1993, 1:55

FULL-COLOR REFERENCE GUIDES TO DIE-CAST EMERGENCY VEHICLES

Volkswagen T4 Caravelle #834, Feuerwehr, 1993-1997, 1:60

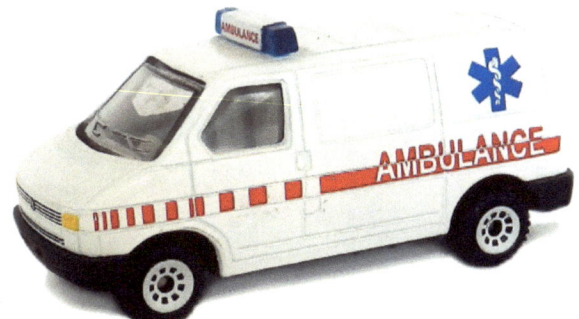

Volkswagen T4 Caravelle #835, Ambulance, 1993-1998, 1:60

Volkswagen T4 Caravelle #835, Ambulance, 1993-1998, 1:60

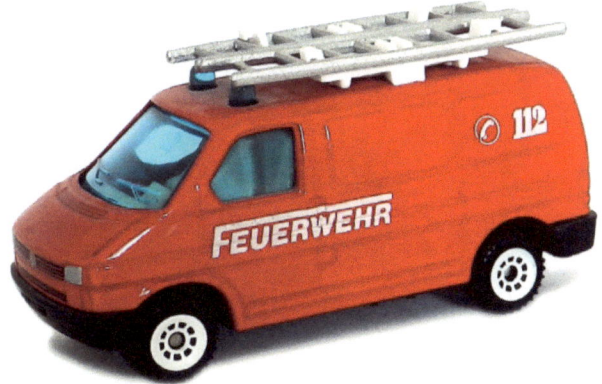

Volkswagen T4 Caravelle #1343, Feuerwehr, 1993-1997, 1:60

MODEL FIRE ENGIES: SIKU

Volkswagen T5 Multivan #1070 (from Emergency Vehicle Set #1821), Feuerwehr, 2008, 1:55

Volkswagen T5 Multivan #1462, Kindernotarzt, 2009-2012, 1:55

Volkswagen T5 Multivan #1462, Kindernotarzt, 2013-2017, 1:55

Volkswagen T5 Multivan #1464/#1460, Feuerwehr, 2012/2013-2017, 1:55

Volvo F12 Fire Station Transporter #4015, 1985-1989, 1:55

MODEL FIRE ENGIES: SIKU

Fire Station #4015, 1985-1989, 1:55

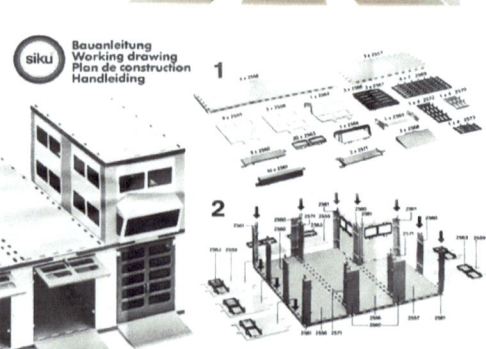
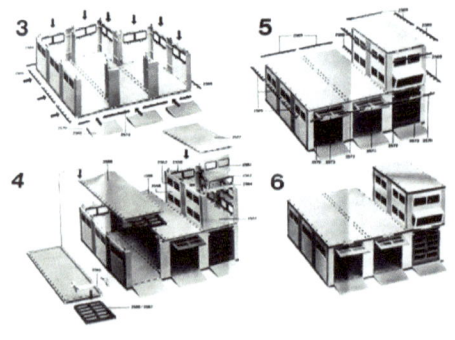

FULL-COLOR REFERENCE GUIDES TO DIE-CAST EMERGENCY VEHICLES

Fire Station #5502, Siku World, 2015-2017, 1:55

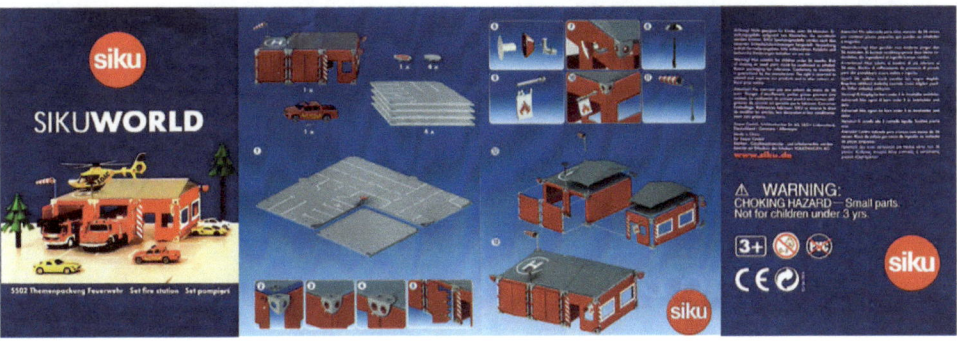

MODEL FIRE ENGIES: SIKU

FULL-COLOR REFERENCE GUIDES TO DIE-CAST EMERGENCY VEHICLES

MODEL FIRE ENGIES: SIKU

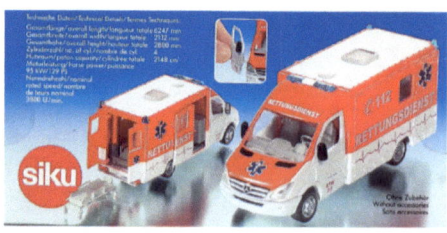

FULL-COLOR REFERENCE GUIDES TO DIE-CAST EMERGENCY VEHICLES

Fire Engine
#121, 1951, 1:60 (plastic)

Mercedes-Benz/Metz LF15 Fire Engine
#F204 (Airport Series), 1959, 1:250 (plastic)

Mercedes-Benz/Metz LF15 Fire Engine
#V55, 1956-1964, 1:60 (plastic)

Mercedes-Benz/Metz DL22 Fire Engine
#V56, 1956-1966, 1:60 (plastic)

Motorrad Gespann, ADAC-Straßenwacht
#V440, 1955-1958, 1:60 (plastic)

Siku Boxes, 1960s-2010s

INDEX

1	Audi (7)
2	BMW (7)
4	Dodge (3)
5	Eurocopter (21)
10	Faun (4)
11	Ford (8)
13	Hako (1)
13	Liebherr (1)
14	Lamborghini (2)
14	Magirus (3)
15	Man (6)
16	Mercedes-Benz (87)
38	Metz/Faun (2)
39	Opel (1)
39	Porsche (4)
40	Range Rover (1)
40	Rosenbauer (6)
42	Scania (4)
43	Smart Car (1)
43	Toyota (2)
43	Volkswagen (29)
51	Volvo (1)

Siku Firefighters, #V407, #V410, 1960

APPENDIX

The models in this Appendix were not included in the first edition of *Model Fire Engines: Siku*.

60	Audi (1)
60	BMW (1)
60	Eurocopter (3)
61	Ford (1)
61	GHE-O (1)
61	Iveco (1)
62	Man (1)
62	Mercedes-Benz (4)
63	Scania (3)
64	Volkswagen (1)

For future updates (including new Siku releases) and information about other books in this series, please visit **www.ModelFireEngines.com.**

MODEL FIRE ENGIES: SIKU

Audi Q7 4.2 FSI Quattro #1429, Ärztefunknotdienst, 2008-2017, 1:55

BMW 5ER Touring #1461, Notarzt, 2017, 1:55

Eurocopter Helicopter BO-105 #2222, Securite Civile, 1986-1997, 1:55

Eurocopter Helicopter BO-105 #2224 (from Lowboy Set #3719), ADAC, 1990-1994, 1:55

FULL-COLOR REFERENCE GUIDES TO DIE-CAST EMERGENCY VEHICLES

Eurocopter BO-105 Helicopter #832, 1993-1995, 1:110

Ford Transit Van #V323, 1971-1974, 1:60

GHE-O Rescue #2307, 2019, 1:60

Iveco/Magirus Multistar Telescopic Platform #1749, 2020, 1:87

Man Aerial Ladder with Platform #2114, 2019, 1:50

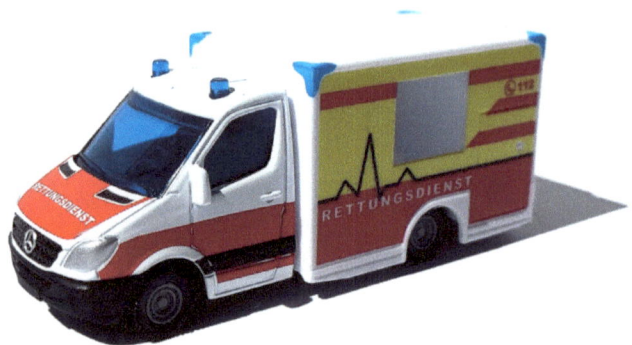

Mercedez-Benz #1536, 2020, 1:87

Mercedes-Benz 280GE with Trailer #2221, ADAC-Straßendienst, 1983-2000, 1:55

Mercedes-Benz G65 AMG #2306, 2019, 1:50

FULL-COLOR REFERENCE GUIDES TO DIE-CAST EMERGENCY VEHICLES

Mercedes-Benz Sprinter Command Car #181800100, 2019, 1:87

Scania Elevating Rescue Platform #1080, 2020, 1:60

Scania Fire Engine #103600300, 2019, 1:87

MODEL FIRE ENGIES: SIKU

Scania Fire Engine #1015, 2019, 1:87

Volkswagon Amarok #1467, 2019, 1:60

for information about updates, new releases and other books in this series:
www.ModelFireEngines.com

Model Fire Engines
Full-Color Reference Guides to Die-Cast Emergency Vehicles

NOW AVAILABLE
Model Fire Engines: Conrad
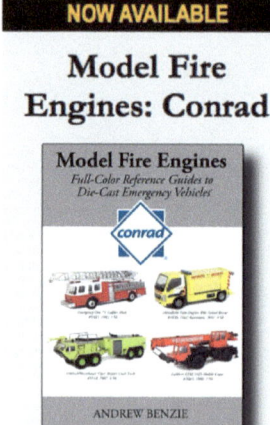

NOW AVAILABLE
Model Fire Engines: Siku
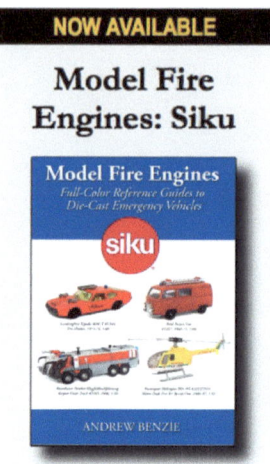

NOW AVAILABLE
Model Fire Engines: Tomica
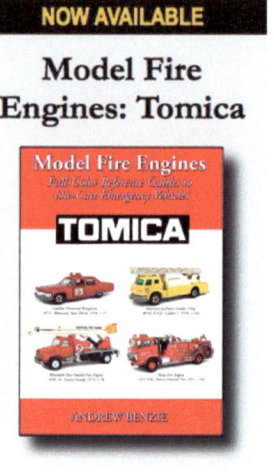

all books available at:
www.ModelFireEngines.com
amazon
and other bookstores

More titles coming soon.
Join mailing list: www.ModelFireEngines.com

About the Author
Author Andrew Benzie began collecting model emergency vehicles in the 1970s when his grandparents gave him his first Corgi and Dinky toy fire engines. Andrew currently lives in the San Francisco Bay Area where he runs a design and book publishing company, and plays bass and drums with several local bands.

FIREHOUSE REPLICAS
& MODEL FIRE STATION TOYS

A MUST-HAVE FOR FIREFIGHTERS AND COLLECTORS OF FIREFIGHTING TOYS!

THE PERFECT BOOK FOR THE FIREHOUSE KITCHEN TABLE.

This long-awaited book (the fourth title published in the author's *Model Fire Engines* series) is the definitive resource for model fire station toys and scale firehouse replicas. Packed full of detailed information, this coffee-table book includes more than 1,000 color images of over 200 scale firehouses and hundreds of die-cast model fire engines. Includes training towers, burning buildings, firefighting figures, and dioramas of Mack's fire engine assembly plant and FDNY's fleet services facility.

Model fire station toys include details about manufacturers and production dates, and firehouse replicas include historical information about each building such as year built, companies quartered, and neighborhoods served *(in New York City, Chicago, Boston, Los Angeles, and many other cities)*.

Featuring firehouses by Code 3 Collectibles, Corgi Classics, Dinky Toys, First Due Firehouse Replicas, Hot Wheels, LEGO, Majorette, Matchbox, Plasticville, Road Champs, Siku, Solido, Tomica, Tootsietoy, and many others. This beautifully designed book will appeal to firefighters, collectors, and children alike. Available in hardcover and softcover.

200+ FIREHOUSES, 200+ PAGES, 1,000+ IMAGES, FULL COLOR

Fire Station including apparatus (plastic), Galoob Micro Machines City Scenes #6468, USA, 1989

FDNY Engine 10/Ladder 10 "The Tenhouse" (hand-painted resin), Code 3 Collectibles #13109, USA, 2004, 1:64

for information about other books in this series:
www.ModelFireEngines.com

ANDREW BENZIE BOOKS

www.ingramcontent.com/pod-product-compliance
Lightning Source LLC
Chambersburg PA
CBHW042029150426
43199CB00002B/14